I dont care what "expert" has this documented wherever !!!

IT'S A FAKE !!!!

And sotheby's let this slip by and did not question it? F-ck the provenance., you can determine visually it's totally wrong !!!! and with all the factual evidence I am providing, it is now made crystal clear.

sold for 4.5 million. I hope the buyer sees this evidence.

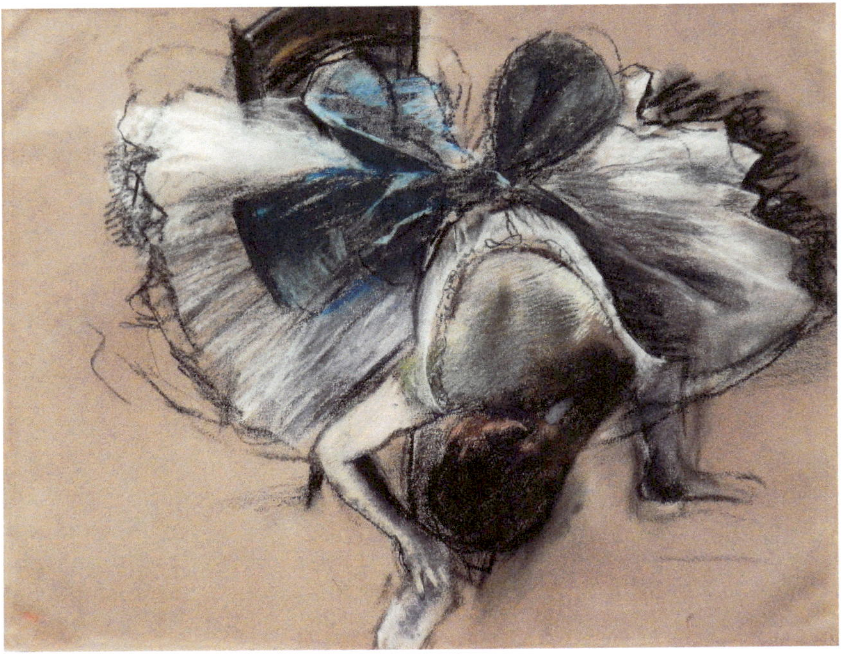

In this short publication is the exposure of five fakes that were sold as Edgar Degas originals, As you can see the evidence presented with my rebuttals, there is quite overwhelming evidence they are not Genuine.
There are no chapters, no preface and no "about the author".
I wrote about my Genuine Degas if you would like to see a REAL one,
https://www.amazon.com/dp/B084QKTYF8
We certainly have a lot of forgeries out there being sold why can't the experts detect them sooner? In this book you will see some of my theories of how deep this may go with Criminal Intent ,,the works artist Edgar Degas they certainly do have a big Supply and where is it coming from? I have provided the factual evidence what this artist type style and media but yet they are selling something to the contrary for decades.
if sombody shall want to put a claim against me for revealing forgeries then let us bring this matter before a jury and im sure it can be sorted all out just fine..

We certainly have a lot of forgeries out there being sold why can't the experts detect them sooner? I imagine it pays very well to look the other way. In this book you will see some of my thoughts of how deep this may go with Criminal Intent the artist of Edgar Degas they certainly do have a big Supply and where is it coming from? I have provided the factual evidence what this artist type style and media but yet they are selling something to the contrary for decades

It is now feb 17th 2020, and I stayed up most the night thinking about the forged artwork and how it was accepted as genuine, It appears that some VERY crafty clever fraudster created a provenance on this "DANSEUSE RAJUSTANT SON CHAUSSON" going back to 1917, and then it has been documented in two books. In my mind the only way this FAKE could keep being documented is if the "expert fraudster" had a friend or relative or business partner(s) to continue this documentation for the following decades. Because (an expert) could not be so stupid to mistake this for an original Degas. Now leads to the next reasonable cause which is>>how many more fakes did they document?.
,,,,,,,,,,,**The "auction house" and "artworld" fictitious requirement of "provenance" makes artworks genuine. This lie circulated and repeated over and over again has become an accepted truth in the subconsious mind.** As I see the very meticulous documentation on the work on the next pages is how it might have been accepted as genuine. And then we have the "experts" who are supposed to be able to spot a forgery and investigate,,,,,,,,,,,,,,,,,, **WERE IS THIER EXPERTISE? How could they miss this one ??** Unless they're in on the game. It's so very very strange these "experts" and auction houses absolutely refuse to accept my Edgar Degas mixed media, it's like they shut me down cold. They dont even want to see it up close and they slam the door like it's such an unwanted reproduction or whatever else they call it. Well it may be quite evident they dont want the genuine Degas to shed relevance on the forgeries as we all know

the museums were buying forgeries "with fake provinances" and the artworld and auction houses are becoming flooded with forgeries. ==The materials analysis is revealing the the forensic evidence,,, so shouldnt this be now the requirement of authentication ??.== Which begs the question, How many forgeries have actually been sold the past 100 years and now they are getting caught more and more. When will it stop ?? and why are the experts and specialists lacking in thier responsibilities ?? Who is the "expert" at sotheby's that allowed that hideous work to be sold in 2013?. I think I could scribble something like that myself. The claim of "Executed in 1887 ", I think that claim ought to be compared to the FACTS !! because Degas WAS NOT creating drawn pastels in that time of his career, and this is totally out of the realm of Degas repertoire. Certainly this very sloppy dis-proportioned ballereina does not reflect his trained skills.

A man with a genuine Picasso was shut down for 12 years by the artworld and auction houses., Here is the link for article below.

https://www.nydailynews.com/new-york/new-jersey-man-believes-find-long-lost-picasso-article-1.2441965

An expert at Christie's in New York dismissed Sabatino's version as a cheap knock-off when she met him at his lawyer's office shortly after the sewing machine discovery, he said.

"She examined it for about 30 seconds and literally flipped it back at me and said, 'This is a $10 poster, don't waste your time,'" he recalled.

"I said, 'Okay, but where did it come from in your opinion? It's in color,'" he recalled.

Color photography and printing were exotic mediums in war-plagued Europe at that time, he said.

"She gave me a deer-in-the-headlights look. She didn't have an answer," he said of the Christie's expert.

So my thoughts are summed up by stating this belief that the auction-artworld has us to believe,,,,,,,,,,,,,,,,,,,,,,,,,,,,,,,,,They are the only ones with Genuine artworks, and the (public's) private collector's and dealer's are all not genuine. Oh is that how it is. Well we see now how the so clever auction houses and artworld is fucking itself because there's just TOO many fakes they cant even keep up with them ALL !!!,. and what more is to become with thier "set of self-engineered rules". Lets look at some correct rules and guidelines for authenticating artwork below of which the experts do not use,,,,,,,I guess because theres too much profits involved with the forgery business.

STANDARDS & GUIDELINES » CAA GUIDELINES

AUTHENTICATIONS AND ATTRIBUTIONS

Adopted by the CAA Board of Directors on October 25, 2009.

A. INTRODUCTION

1. One of the areas of great responsibility, and great controversy, for art historians, whether they are employed by an academic institution or a museum, or operate as independent scholars or experts, is that of authenticating or attributing works of art. If art historians choose to engage in the practice of authentication (stating the artwork is or is not by a particular artist) or attribution (identifying the artist), it is very important that they be aware of the issues involved.1

2. Issues of attribution and authentication differ substantially among the various fields of art history, including to name just a few, Greek pottery, Chinese bronzes and paintings, Roman copies of Greek sculpture, Indian sculpture, medieval sculpture, Mesoamerican artifacts in general, old-master paintings in particular, nineteenth-century landscape and genre works, and works of modern and contemporary art passim. In many fields there may only be one or two experts capable of giving an informed opinion. In others there may be many experts and conflicting published opinions. In modern and contemporary art, it is sometimes difficult to identify an expert at all, to the extent that artists may not have a catalogue raisonné or scholarly monograph to indicate which authors or editors would be the acknowledged experts.

3. Although many art historians continue to issue individual opinions about attribution or authenticity, due to possible risks of litigation over the rendering of opinions, these guidelines recommend a different approach. Furthermore, given the international context in which opinions are rendered, international legal issues, including those relating to ownership and libel, must be approached with caution and legal guidance.

4. "Certificate" opinions concerning or implying authentication or attribution, given for business, market-value, or tax purposes, no longer, in all circumstances, represent infallible objectivity unless they are supported by a consensus. It is recommended that art historians be very cautious about issuing such opinions solely on their own authority alone.

B. RECOMMENDED PRACTICES

1. It is recommended that art historians render opinions only on artworks that are within their competence. In particular, it is recommended that art historians render opinions, when possible, in conjunction with a group of other scholars and conservators who can form a consensus as to the authenticity or attribution of an artwork.

2. It is recommended that art historians rely on specialists employing technologically sophisticated analytical techniques for the material analysis of objects.

3. **Art-historical documentation, stylistic connoisseurship, and technical or scientific analysis, which complement each other, are the three necessary aspects of best practices for authentication and attribution.** These three aspects create a consensus of evidence. A consensus of evidence is, in itself, the best approach to authentication and attribution and the best defense against litigation. In forming a consensus, the experts involved should be sensitive to the damage a publicized negative opinion can do to the reputation of an owner and the value of the art object.

4. Those asked to express an opinion on an artwork's authenticity or attribution are advised to study the original artwork itself before rendering an opinion, although there may be instances where an opinion may be rendered on the basis of a photograph (as when the artwork is unavailable or a blatant fake). The opinion should indicate whether it is based on a study of the artwork or a photograph. In any event, relevant data, including media, dimensions, location, and mode of signature, should be obtained and carefully verified, as well as any inscriptions on the backing of the work (its verso and stretcher). The opinion should be labeled as such and should include the relevant identification data in describing the artwork, including photographic images taken from the original.

5. Art historians who face a situation that precludes establishing a consensus are advised to use caution, should consider whether to withdraw from the assignment, and/or should consult legal counsel.

6. It is recommended that an art historian employed by an institution first consult that institution to determine whether, and on what conditions or restrictions, he or she may render opinions with respect to the authenticity or attribution of works of art. It must also be determined if that institution insures the art historian with respect to such opinions. As a general rule, it is inappropriate for an art historian to render opinions on the letterhead of his or her institution without the knowledge and consent of the institution. Some institutions have devised forms and procedures for the rendering of opinions in order to minimize the risks of, or avoid, litigation. Where such insurance arrangements, forms, and procedures exist, they should be scrupulously followed. Any questions should be referred to the institution's legal officer.

7. It is recommended that an independent art historian not render an authentication or attribution opinion absent insurance, indemnification, and a signed release of all claims by the owner of the work.

8. It is recommended that when an art historian encounters an artwork in a museum that he or she believes to be misattributed, his or her opinion should be communicated privately, not publicly, to the appropriate curator. Where the artwork is not owned or exhibited by a museum, the art historian should not get involved unless asked for an opinion.

9. It is recommended that when an art historian encounters an artwork in a commercial gallery that he or she believes to be misattributed, he or she should render an opinion only if asked to do so and is indemnified, inasmuch as it may not be possible to obtain a signed release of all claims by the owner of the work (or the gallery) once an opinion has already been rendered.

10. It is recommended that opinions be rendered for collectors only when there is a written request by the owner of the work, and that the owner provides all parties involved in rendering the opinion with a release signed by the owner and appropriate indemnification. An art historian rendering an opinion may wish to consult a lawyer regarding the elements of such a release.

11. It is recommended that an opinion on authentication or attribution not be offered unless the owner of the work provides sufficient scholarly research and technical evidence to support the opinion.

12. It is recommended that an opinion avoid commenting on the character or reputation of the seller or owner of an artwork. With respect to those cases where an art historian has reason to doubt or disagree with a proffered attribution, an opinion of "misattribution" or "not properly attributed to" is appropriate, unless it is clear that the work is a forgery. Finally, the art historian should retain for his or her own records a copy of the opinion, the release, an image of the work, and all relevant correspondence.

C. ETHICAL ISSUES

1. Although every art historian must be aware of professional responsibilities of acting on his or her expertise, there is no obligation to act individually or publicly—or to put oneself and one's family in harm's way.

2. It is unethical for an art historian to provide an opinion of a known fake or forgery that affirms the legitimacy of its authenticity or attribution.

3. It is unethical for an art historian to "authenticate" artworks through publicity to form public opinion.

4. It is unethical for a museum to organize or sponsor an exhibition of artworks as to which the authenticity or attribution is open to question unless the doubts are clearly indicated or the exhibition is openly devoted to assist in the determination of attributions or to presenting forgeries or misattributions.

5. In rendering an opinion, it is recommended not to charge a fee, unless circumstances would not be compromised by doing so. One exception to this recommendation would be if the artwork is authentic, published in a catalogue raisonné, and has never been questioned, and if the request is clearly for an affirmation of authentication. Other exceptions would be fees paid to technical experts such as conservators, who are part of a consensus issuing an opinion, and fees paid to authentication committees constituted by artists' foundations or similar institutions.

COMMENTARY

The above guidelines constitute revisions of **A Code of Ethics for Art Historians and Guidelines for the Professional Practice of Art History**: Section VI, "Fakes and Forgeries," and Code of Ethics: Section X, "Fakes and Forgeries." Both parts titled "Fakes and Forgeries" have been included in Section XI, whose title has been changed to "Authentications and Attributions" from just "Attributions."

NOTES

1. These guidelines distinguish between forgeries, which are purposeful misrepresentations of an artist's work that most often contain a fraudulent signature, and works that were not intentionally made as representations of another's work but were mistaken for it. The former are inauthentic; the latter are most often misattributions.

AUTHORS AND CONTRIBUTORS

These guidelines are submitted by the Task Force on Authentication, authorized by the CAA Board of Directors in October 2008, that consisted of:

- Barbara B. Lynes, Director, Georgia O'Keeffe Museum Research Center, and Curator, Georgia O'Keeffe Museum, Santa Fe, New Mexico
- Francis V. O'Connor (Task Force Chair), former member of the Pollock-Krasner Authentication Board and its predecessors
- Meg Perlman, former Director of the Pollock-Krasner House and Study Center at East Hampton, New York
- Virginia Rutledge, attorney and member of CAA's Committee on Intellectual Property and Chair of the New York City Bar Association's Art Law Committee
- Ronald D. Spencer, attorney and member of the New York City Bar Association's Art Law Committee, counsel to the Pollock-Krasner and Andy Warhol Foundations, and author of The Expert versus the Object: Judging Fakes and False Attributions in the Visual Arts (New York: Oxford University Press, 2004)

who has the authority and power to get these fake artworks documented? the "experts". who can fabricate such fake provenances ? the "experts". And who can create such bull shit "cover-up" stories? the "experts". Seems they have it under control but not for long, because karma is catching up with them. Oh what a tangled web of lies they weave, when they lie, cheat, & steal to DECIEVE !!

So where is the "Art Police"? And maybe this is why they are getting away with it for so long and laughing all the way to the bank. I have reported these fakes to numorous authorities who have not responded. Recently the FBI tells me they only investigate stolen artworks. Thats nice, but millions of $$ in forgeries can be sold and thats ok with them, I guess they dont have any real art experts to examine all these works being sold, We also need a language expert to analyse the sentence structure of these very shrewd writers of their "hype" mis-truths and very misleading statements.

==Is somebody claiming that something is real, let them prepare an affidavit of Truth and swear to it under penalty of perjury before a public notary.== If somebody suggests something is genuine and they cannot prove it, therefore this takes no expertise and anybody can make such a suggestion. But the expertise comes in the form of manipulative words and hype created by professional writers to give people the illusion that it's genuine as I see the wording on many artworks for sale and the disclosure is very very clever and releasing the seller from liability. (in some instances). The real expertise I see is the deception with the sales pitches and the Provenance that's added which is clearly has to be faked. I really cannot push the blame on the people for being ignorant, as they are surely being conned by professionals

Edgar Degas spontenaeity & complex media

"If a painting were not so difficult, then it would not be so much fun"
Edgar Degas quote

I assure you no art was ever less spontaneous than mine. What I do is the result of reflection and study of the great masters; of inspiration, spontaneity, temperament — temperament is the word — I know nothing.

- Said in conversation with George Moore and quoted by Moore in *Impressions and Opinions* (1891)

What a delightful thing is the conversation of specialists! One understands absolutely nothing and it's charming.
- Quoted in a letter by Daniel Halévy (1892-01-31), from *Degas Letters,* ed. Marcel Guerin, trans. Marguerite Kay (1947)

I'm glad to say I haven't found my style yet. I'd be bored to death.
- "Technical Details" (p. 70)

- You must do over the same subject ten times, a hundred times. In art nothing must appear accidental, even a movement.

  because of the many tracings that **Degas** did of his drawings, the public accused him of repeating himself. But his passion for perfection was responsible for this continual research.
- w:Ambroise Vollard, in *Degas*, George Allen and Unwin, 1928

[**Degas** compared] to a writer striving to attain the utmost precision of form, drafting and redrafting, canceling, advancing by endless recapitulation, never admitting that his work has reached its *final* stage: from sheet to sheet, copy to copy, he continually revises his drawing, deepening, tightening, closing it up.

- w: Paul Valéry, in *Degas, Manet, Morisot*, Princeton, Princeton University 1989; as quoted in *Outside the Lines*, David W. Galenson, Harvard University Press, 2001, p. 89
"a technician who experimented greatly"

In an article written by studio international, National Gallery of London states;
  "Given the Gallery's holdings of works by Edgar Degas, one would have expected to find numerous examples of his works there. It was, however, the sheer variety and complexity in Degas's *oeuv re,* and the wide range of methods and materials employed that led curators at the National Gallery to consider Degas a special case. Instead of using their collection of his work in their important 1991 exhibition, a decision was made to do significantly more research and to assemble, from museums and galleries from around the world, a truly comprehensive exhibition of Degas's work."

"pastel was important indeed pivotal for degas for whom experimentation re- working intense pure pigment, were vital he took up photography to achieving masterful images with light and shade Degas personally enigmatic and technically complex"

reference link
http://www.studiointernational.com/index.php/art-in-the-making-degas

----

"His mastery of technique was superb, and he experimented with various media including pastel"

reference link
https://www.nationalgallery.org.uk/artists/hilaire-germain-edgar-degas

---

"However, Degas would endlessly experiment with unusual techniques. He would sometimes mix his pastel so heavily with liquid fixative that it became amalgamated into a sort of paste. He would do a drawing in charcoal and use layers of pastel to cover part of this. He would combine pastels and oil in a single work"

reference link
http://www.degas-painting.info/degasstyle.htm

"Degas was interested in mining the countless possibilities from a single image."

"Degas studio was like a laboratory"

reference link
https://www.moma.org/momaorg/shared/pdfs/docs/publication_pdf/3230/Degas_StrangeNewBeauty_PREVIEW.pdf

---

Renoir stated that; "Degas would lay a drawing on the floor, cover it with a board, and stomp on it to grind in the pastel into the paper" and Degas said he has not yet found his method, that would only bore him !!

Degas created over 700 pastels, more than in any other medium that he explored. **Always a restless experimenter, Degas pushed the medium to its expressive limits.**

Degas's technical mastery of pastels was unsurpassed. **Aware that some pastel colorants fade when exposed to light, Degas put his pastels out in the sun to bleach fugitive colorants out of them before he used them. He often used pastel moistened with water and mixed with an adhesive such as casein, creating a kind of pastel paste that gave the appearance of paint applied with a brush. He even selectively moistened pastel passages with steam or a spray of boiling water and then extended the dissolved pastel with a brush into a translucent layer of color or pastel paste.** Degas's friends report seeing him place a drawing on the ground, cover it with board, and stomp on it to grind the pastel into the paper.

reference link

http://blog.phillipscollection.org/2011/12/20/degas-and-pastels-part-i/

These media types were used by Degas from mid 1870s to1890s !!
Media may include but not limited to: **(on my Edgar Degas work)**
egg tempera, distemper, gouache, encaustic, wet and dry pastel, wet pastel consisting of glue base and or sprayed with boiling water, turpentine thinned oil paints [essence], and also lavender oil>>thinned oil paints [essence], oil paint with the oil squeezed out of it bringing it back to dry pigment then re-mixing it with other pigments and chemicals, home made soap,>>

[glycerin+soda+water] water color, beeswax mixed with oil paints, 2 types of fixative; one was white shellac mixed with methyl alcohol, the other was borax mixed with casein and water, fermented for a few days then mixed with methyl alcohol.

possible media learned from Mary Cassatt, such as metallic

-
- Make a drawing. Start it all over again, trace it. Start it and trace it again.
- You must do over the same subject ten times, a hundred times. In art nothing must appear accidental, even a movement.
-
- [**Degas** compared] to a writer striving to attain the utmost precision of form, drafting and redrafting, canceling, advancing by endless recapitulation, never admitting that his work has reached its *final* stage: from sheet to sheet, copy to copy, he continually revises his drawing, deepening, tightening, closing it up.
-
- I have often heard **Degas** say that in painting you must give the idea of the true by means of the false.
-
-
- Walter Sickert, "The Royal Academy," *English Review* (June 1912)
- because of the many tracings that **Degas** did of his drawings, **the public accused him of repeating**

himself. But his passion for perfection was responsible for this continual research.
-
-
- I am convinced that **Degas** felt a work could never be called *finished*, and that he could not conceive how an artist could look at one of his pictures after a time and not feel the need to retouch it.
- w: Paul Valéry, in *Degas, Manet, Morisot*, Princeton, Princeton University 1989; as quoted in *Outside the Lines*, David W. Galenson, Harvard University Press, 2001, p. 89
- Severely self-critical, he would take a certain pleasure in repeating what a critic had said about him in a review of an exhibition: Continually uncertain about proportions.[mine is larger than the pink one], Nothing, he [= **Degas**] claimed, could better describe his state of mind while he was toiling and struggling over a work.

FAKES

we're going to look at some evidence now of what I found as I have seen over 1000 Degas artworks and studied his technique, habits & personality.
And this evidence I'm going to show you I believe a jury would come to the same conclusion that these 3 artworks WERE NOT created by the hands of Edgar Degas. Which now begs the question why these "experts" represented them as genuine, and how did they ever get documented with their FAKE provenance? And where are the rest like mine?? Just WTF is going on out there in the art world?? Degas was GETTING BORED with traditional pastels and in the early 1870s, (I think he started his experimenting earlier than what is told by sources) he was concocting many mixtures and pre-sun-bleaching his colors, which means they were NOT traditional pastel colors.

http://www.sothebys.com/en/auctions/ecatalogue/2013/impressionist-modern-art-evening-sale-l13002/lot.19.html

Larger image can be seen in the link. Whos the pig who created the artwork in the first pic below? Her ass isn't even in the chair !! Degas was well studied on the human anatomy and body motion & proportion. So why is the bow exceedingly oversized? The edges of the dress are very sloppy, unlike all the other dress trims I've seen. The back and neck is not in the correct position, the lower left leg is as if it is still in a "sketch" state and not completed. Left arm position is totally wrong. And this was created in 1887????? when Degas was very heavily into experimenting with pastel MIXTURES by that time. And WHAT TYPE of paper was this on ?? I'll get to the paper in the next chapter, So anyways I ordered both the books below and found the work in question was documented, seems like an airtight provenance, I wonder how it was done? Because that piece of shit was NOT done by Edgar Degas. Degas would go to customer's homes taking back artworks to re-touch them and make them more perfect. Degas' strive for his own uniqueness and mastery of the dancer would never be presented like a amateur scribble !!

Paul-André Lemoisne, *Degas et son œuvre*, Paris, 1946, vol. III, no. 907, illustrated p. 529
Robert Gordon & Andrew Forge, *Degas*, New York, 1988, illustrated in colour p. 193
PROPERTY FROM A PRIVATE EUROPEAN COLLECTION

I'LL TELL YA WHAT FOLKS, IF THESE PROVENANCES ARE BEING FAKED BACK IN THE 19TH CENTURY AND ARTWORKS LIKE THESE BEING DOCUMENTED in the 1940s by more "experts", THERE IS A VERY VERY VERY SERIOUS PROBLEM !!!, And they paid 4.5 million because a major auction house had it with these fabricated provenances ? Is that the game ?

"Counterfeiters have never had more tools at their disposal than they do today," he explains. "Technology has made it a lot easier to create counterfeit works and also provenance documents that back up the works. You have incredibly sophisticated fraudsters who are outright fabricating ostensibly authenticated works of art. If you think of the tools that a graphic designer has in this day and age in the hands of an art fraudster, the realities come into focus. Technology is making it easier to forge and counterfeit."

http://thecreatorsproject.vice .com/blog/art-crime-detectives

Edgar Degas
Paul-André Lemoisne, *Degas et son œuvre*,

Paris, 1946, vol. III **Edgar Degas**1834 – 1917

DANSEUSE RAJUSTANT SON CHAUSSON PROPERTY FROM A PRIVATE EUROPEAN COLLECTION

Edgar Degas
DANSEUSE RAJUSTANT SON CHAUSSON
Estimate3,000,000 — 5,000,000 GBP**LOT SOLD.** 4,521,250 GBP

stamped *Degas* (lower left)

pastel on paper

50 by 62.5cm.

19 5/8 by 24 5/8 in.

Executed in 1887.READ CONDITION REPORTSALEROOM NOTICE

PROVENANCE

Sale: Galerie Georges Petit, Paris, *Atelier Edgar Degas, 2ème Vente*, 11th-13th December 1918, lot 191
Nunès et Fiquet, Paris
Roger G. Gompel, Paris
Private Collection, Europe (acquired from the above)

EXHIBITED

Paris, Galerie Bernheim-Jeune, *Exposition de cent ans de théâtre, music-hall et cirque*, 1936, no. 29
(titled *Dansueuse assise rajustant sa chaussure*)

Paris, Musée de l'Orangerie, *Degas*, 1937, no. 138
Paris, La Gazette des Beaux-Arts, *Degas dans les collections Françaises*, 1955, no. 123, illustrated in the catalogue (titled *Danseuse remettant sa sandale* and as dating from 1886)

LITERATURE   Did Paul Brame publish the book below?, I found a couple on google

Paul-André Lemoisne, *Degas et son œuvre*, Paris, 1946, vol. III, no. 907, illustrated p. 529
Robert Gordon & Andrew Forge, *Degas*, New York, 1988, illustrated in colour p. 193

degas et son oeuvre by lemoisne paul andre - - Biblio.com
www.biblio.com › Booksearch

1.
Results 1 - 8 of 8 - **Degas et son oeuvre** EDITION ORIGINALE by **LEMOISNE Paul-André**. **Paris**: Plon, 1954. ... **Paris**: Paul Brame **and** C.M. **De** Hauke, 1949. ... **Vol**. 2: xiii, 407 pp. 716 + bw photographs. Vo. **3**: pp. 407-839, photographs 717-1466. ... **1946** . (**Degas**, Edgar). DEGAS ET SON OEUVRE by **Paul-Andre Lemoisne**.

Paul-André Lemoisne - Degas et son Oeuvre - 4 volumes - 1946
www.catawiki.com › ... › Book Auction (Art & Photography)

1.
Nov 26, 2017 - **Paul-André Lemoisne - Degas et son Oeuvre** - 4 volumes - **1946** ... **Paul-André Lemoisne**,**Degas et son Oeuvre** Vols I-IV,**Paris**, P. Brame **and** C.M. **De** Hauke, **1946** ... after **Degas**, **1946**, on wove, each **volume** with justification, title-page, ... The seller will ship the item(s) within **3** working days after receiving ...

FAKE !!, And condition report is unavailable

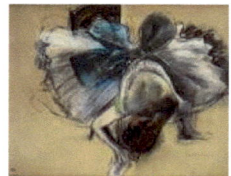

Compare the fake to the pics on next pages, and there's plenty more for comparison on google images.

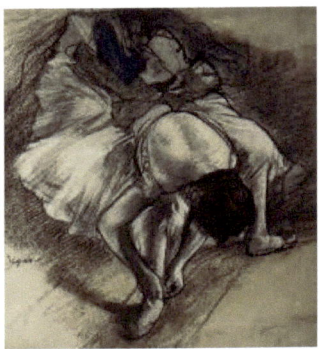

Compare the bow proportions, the left legs, the edges of dress, the position of the back, What would a jury believe? This is very disturbing to discover this fake that was EVEN accompanied by the fake engineered provenance , I know a lot more also, but lets stick to the obvious for the time.

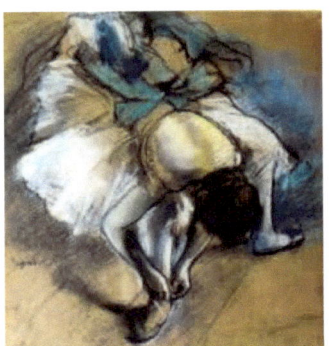

On this one above, her ass is in the chair !!

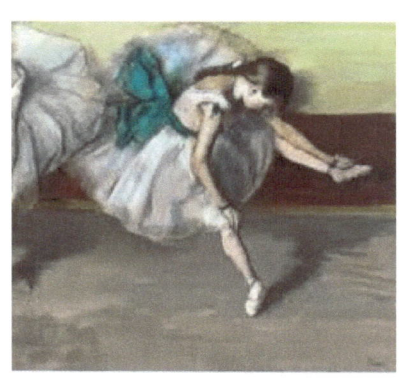

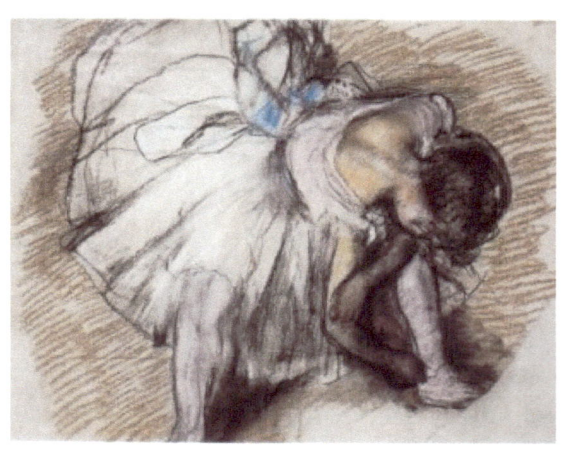

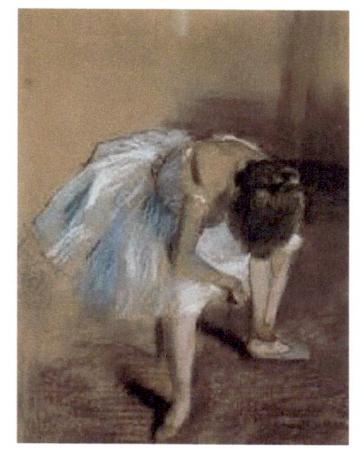

These two are seated in the chair properly, legs are finished and not roughly sketched. edges of dresses not scribbled, Degas created refined finished exquisite works,,,,,,,,**not** SLOPPY SCRIBBLES totally misaligned

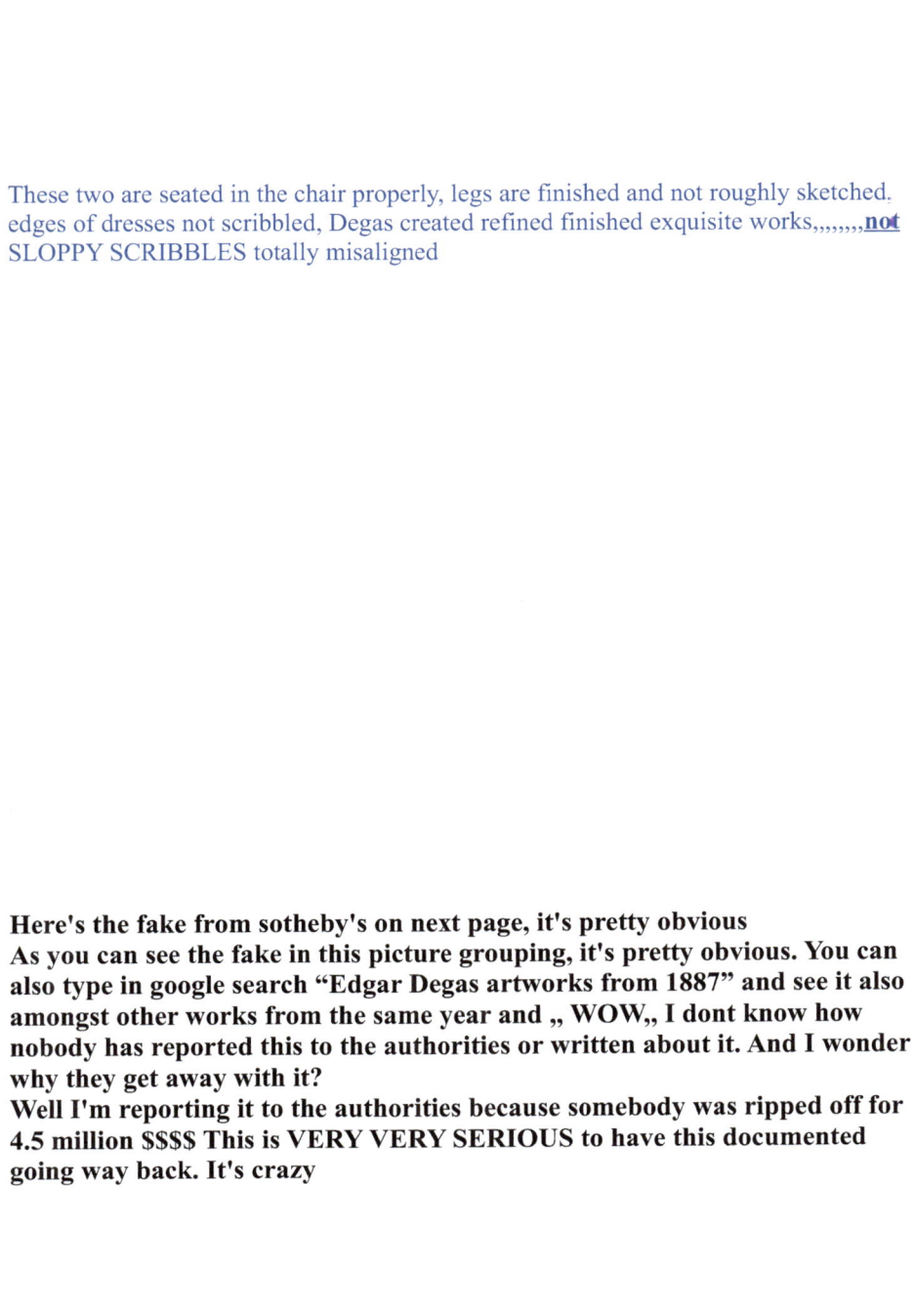

Here's the fake from sotheby's on next page, it's pretty obvious
As you can see the fake in this picture grouping, it's pretty obvious. You can also type in google search "Edgar Degas artworks from 1887" and see it also amongst other works from the same year and ,, WOW,, I dont know how nobody has reported this to the authorities or written about it. And I wonder why they get away with it?
Well I'm reporting it to the authorities because somebody was ripped off for 4.5 million $$$$ This is VERY VERY SERIOUS to have this documented going way back. It's crazy

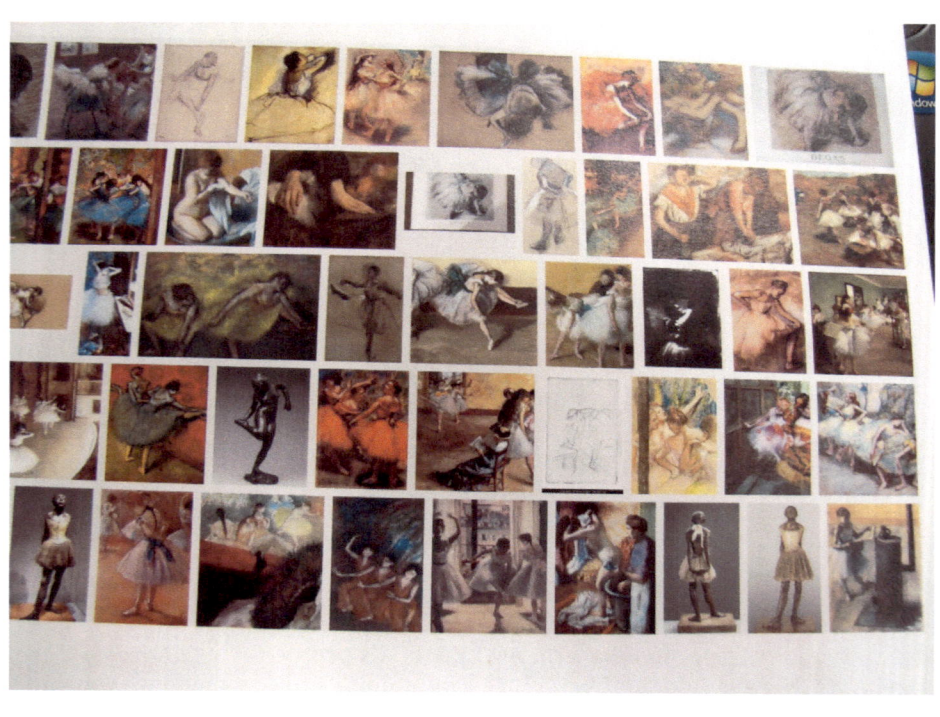

Do a google search, "Edgar Degas artworks from 1887" and compare the works

At least mine isnt all scribbled up !!!

And dont get me wrong, I'm not claiming ALL Degas' pastels were created with his mixtures, but the evidence is showing that it was his known repertoire that he advanced into. Certainly much too advanced to create scribbly works in traditional color. The ones obvious to the trained eye like myself would notice,

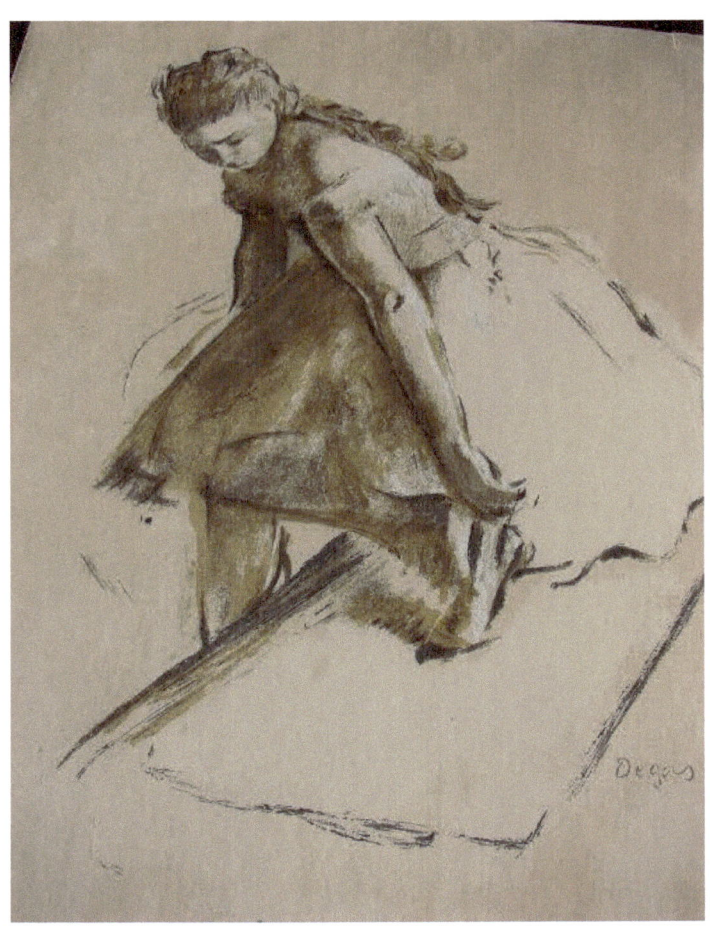

Another fake sold for 450,000 Bonhams in California
Trois danseuses - un dessin rehaussé
Edgar Degas (French, 1834-1917),with highlights, possibly by a later hand
In a French 18th Century carved and decapé gilded frame £400,000 – 600,000,US$ 520,000 – 780,000 Trois danseuses - un dessin rehaussé signed 'Degas' (lower right) charcoal and pastel on paper
54.6 x 42.5cm (21 1/2 x 16 3/4in). In a French 18th Century carved and decapé gilded frame
Executed in 1896>>it may have been, but not by Edgar Degas
https://www.bonhams.com/auctions/16218/lot/23/
Feast your eyes on this masterpiece-OF-SHIT. Nice wording "possibly touched by a later hand"? Really?? it looks like a 10 year old fucked it up with a black crayon ! Haha wheres the reflection of light ? It looks VERY VERY BLAND !! Dancers look ugly !!

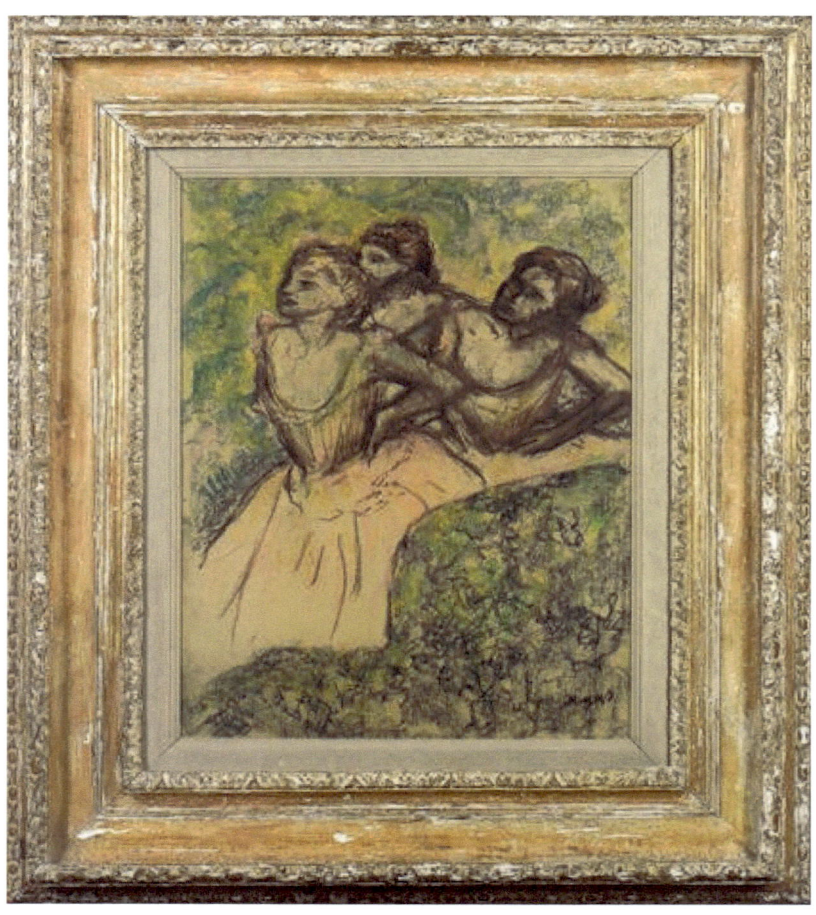

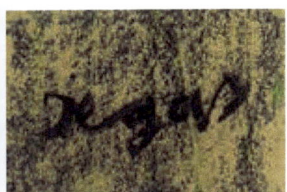

check out this signature !! that letter "a" is not correct, and "D" is too close to the e, the signature isnt even straight, as it has a curvature upwards on the ends. It is not consistant with over 500 signatures i've seen. I emailed Dr Libby twice asking questions and she never responded, so this work was done in 1896? and the reason its such a mess is because they say Degas' old age and eyesight? Degas had too much pride and dignity to let something like this out in public, plus at that time of his life he was well PRACTICED in using "pastel mixtures", !!!!! this one claims just a "red lead mixed into pink" , with all the facts & evidence I have provided in these facts here in this book AND the broad variety of media Degas was KNOWN TO USE, The facts do not add up that this was executed by him, 20 Years prior Degas was already experimenting heavily with his laboratory created "ONE OF A KIND" mixtures so why would he create such a bland ugly work with no light reflection? And only one mixture found??
Forgers are WELL knowing on which pigments to use. And what a very manipulative use of words below. Its all BULL SHIT. It's called "false and misleading statements" and its illegal the way this "exam" is told.
What type of paper was used? Was there Any X-ray imaging performed to search for a watermark or framework beneath the pastel? Why not? The record of who purchased it from who DOESNT MATTER because this is NOT GENUINE !!!

Dr. Libby Sheldon has examined the work under laboratory conditions. Her findings are as below,

The presence of a fixative layer over the intense black drawing suggests that the green, yellow and pink colours were applied later, **but there is no firm indication of whether they were applied by the artist of the drawing or by a later hand.** What is they?? the green yellow and pink?? if its not a definate proven fact that the colors were not applied by Degas then the entire piece is questionable. And my facts show that Degas was bored with traditional pastel drawing,,,,,,,,,,,,,,,,He painted on his pastel mixtures

The pigments identified in the colours were all those available throughout the last half of the 19th century and there were no anachronistic materials. The greens and yellows have been encountered in works by Degas. Chrome green, (the colourman's combination of chrome yellow and Prussian blue) has been found in use in pastel paintings by Degas; for example it occurs in, 'Russian Dancers', 1899. The Prussian blue element in the pastel 'After the Bath', 1890-5, appears very dark in infra-red, as it does in the painting under discussion (see illustration). *Using the same pigments and colors is what forgers do !! DUH !!*
The finding of red lead mixed into the pink is interesting, *youre a dum ass !!*since it has been found in use on some painted works by Degas, in the National Gallery London, London. Red lead was used rarely by contemporary artists. It has been identified in in an early work by Pissarro of 1874 'Kitchen at Piette's, Montfoucault' (Detroit Institute of Arts), and Callan, quoting this find, remarks on its unusual employment. Crimson lake is a commonly used pigment, as is the type of lead white and chalk also making up the pinks. SO WHAT.

Pigment analysis shows that the additions are likely to have been worked by the same hand that applied the colours to the main image. Their identification also presents a palette range available in the late 19th century,all speculation and NOT FACT.
with no pigments from a later date. *All the pigments used here have been found in works by Degas, and*

the use of red lead is particularly interesting. **WOW !!! REALLY !!!!???**

here we see the black used for the destruction of the fake work and the signature is "similar enough"?? what does that mean?? where is the composition forensics to support that claim of actual material used??

The black of the signature and drawing are similar enough to allow it to have been executed using the same black for both. It has been put on over the colours and fixative but there are *no technical reasons to suggest it was applied by a different hand.'* ?? That signature isnt even close

We are grateful to Dr. Libby Sheldon for this analysis. And fictitious conveyance of words

This is all speculation below, very carefully worded, is it suggesting Degas went mentally retarted and lost his wits??? and created shoddy ugly artworks before his death ?? It's clear to me that a forger created this monstrosity in green,, the facts DO NOT ADD UP, It's not even close to the characteristics and style of what Degas was in the habit of doing very complex works, as the one I own shows clearly with factual evidence gathered by historians and curators of high merit.

What I'm noticing is a continuous pattern of half truths and fabricated fiction mixed in with fractions of truth,,,,, all to sway the belief that something is genuine. This entire provenance and exam can be picked to pieces and discovered that over 60-70% cannot be proven as fact. I suspect a lawliar helped dr libby sheldon prepare this tangled web of misaligned and contradictive misleading statements. Would Dr Libby Sheldon swear under penalty of perjury that her analysis is 100% correct and the Degas here shown is a Genuine work created by Edgar Degas? I seriously doubt it !! Everything Dr. Libby claims is contrary to Facts of Degas' practices & methods and time periods during where Degas became more advanced in his pastel mixtures. He did not go backwards.

it is evident dr libby sheldon is ignorant of Degas methods, **OR** intentionally engineered this manipulative summary of carefully engineered BS. I see this all too often. she shows exitement and gives high credibility to the artwork because of the iron ore red pigment mix, thats very amusing !!!! perhaps she should read my facts report. Edgar Degas **WAS** so far advanced with his complex pastel mixtures by 1917, there was **NO TANGIBLE REASON** to create this work using methods from early in his career at the time of 1855 (approximatley). and like i said ,,, its BLAND and shows NO reflection of light. so what would a jury believe?? could miss sheldon swear under penalty of perjury that this is a genuine Degas work? could she swear that her analysis is 100% correct ? **I HIGHLY DOUBT IT !!** and these shenanigans **DO** exist in the artworld. I could make a career investigating artworks theres so many questionable, as I've shown 2 here in this book. She also stated that Degas "later pastel highlighting may not be typical of Degas' style"?? to add credibility to the piece of shit for the auction company to sell so she gets paid !!

In the 1914 Vollard exhibition catalogue there are quite a few dessins 'rehausses' or re-highlighted works. The work does appear to be in a more basic form in this book, ie without some of the pastel highlighting. There has been a suggestion that some of the later pastel highlighting may not be typical of Degas' style and as stated there is no photograph showing the work in its state between 1914, the date of the Vollard exhibition and 1917, the year Degas died. It is entirely plausible that Degas returned to the work before his death in 1917 and made some further pastel additions really ?? who seen that ?

to create the finished work as we see it now. We do know that the pastel used is typical of that Degas used at the time ,which time? 1850S, 1860s, 1870s, 1880s, 1890s, ?? Degas wasnt hardly using traditional pastels after 1870 from my evidence, he was mixing a broad variety of other media creating his own concoctions !!

so what !!! all forgers know what to use, it's very obvious !! but the forgers could never duplicate a genuine Degas mixture of tempera, or glycerin, or pre sun-bleach pigments mixed with pastel

and we are grateful to Libby Sheldon of the UCL analysis laboratory for confirming this by means of a pastel examination.

Where's the UCL analysis? LETS SEE IT. And how do you know Degas "returned" to the pastel to make "further additions"??? I wonder why he forgot to add the reflection of light, doesnt make any sence that Degas would forget that, and it doeswnt make any sence that he would create such a piece of shit like this one, I'm legally blind myself but correctable with eye glasses. This whole analysis story is total BULL SHIT. Does anyone actually think Degas would do a work like this one for his last artworks to remember him by?? youre crazy !!!!!! AND HE WASNT DRAWING THE PASTEL, HE WAS PAINTING IT ON WITH A BRUSH, he wasnt using traditional colors anymore, he was using MIXTURES he made himself !!!

This work belongs to a series of pastels of varying degrees of finish executed in 1898-1899, many of which were purchased by Degas's dealer Paul Durand-Ruel. We do not know if this work was among them but we do know it was in an exhibition curated by the dealer Ambroise Vollard in 1914. Around the turn of the century Degas was experimenting with his drawings and his pastels, often burnishing his works and using fixative to create dfferent effects. The pastel colours on top of charcoal used here especially the distinctive madder pink are characteristic of Degas' later work. *Correction,, it was 30 years prior to the "turn of the century"*

BRAVO BRAVO !!!!!!., Nice story telling, What I'd like to know is who is making up the fake provenances?? like the fake Degas I exposed prior to this one. It is a VERY VERY SERIOUS PROBLEM TO HAVE PROVENANCE FAKED GOING BACK TO THE 1880s and even "turn of the century". I see the major auction houses have the "fine art" market all under control. Yeah the ones demanding a "provenance" from me and reject and suppress my Edgar Degas mixed media.

I decided to do a search on the auction houses selling fakes and what a field day !!! What I now question is the journalists and media reporters who write some of the stories to remove the guilt and blame and direct it to another reasoning. Just as a lab examiner can be corrupt and fabricate a false analysis, so can a journalist. I dont doubt it for a second.

And in the world of "experts" they'll sell you anything, wines, artifacts, antique rugs, there's plenty of auction houses with experts. But very few of them has been sentenced to jail time which leaves the door wide open to continue what their doing and cover it up with STORIES!!!

More fakes, Christie's sells fakes and I knew the major auction houses were going to fuck thierself, it was just a matter of time. They're way out of control with their "experts" and criminal behaviors. Ant of course they'll keep selling fakes and keep getting caught. It's sickening. It's a continuous pattern now from what I see, just keep selling fakes and pay a settlement when you get caught. Is this what the auction houses have become?? and why they refuse my genuine Degas because it would expose ALL THIER FAKES !!!! I suspect they have a wharehouse somewhere loaded with fakes and some of them the provenance was already created back many years ago as the first one I showed in this chapter. That would mean an organized crime syndicate. Although I cannot prove it, there IS probable cause !!! Check the article below how crafty they are with their disclosure,,,,, as I have also shown with the Bonham's fake examined by Dr. Libby Sheldon with her word trickery.

https://www.smh.com.au/national/nsw/barrister-louise-mcbride-wins-case-against-christies-auction-house-over-fake-albert-tucker-painting-20141204-11zy98.html

Justice Bergin said Ms McBride had made out her case of ==misleading and deceptive conduct by all three parties under the Trade Practices Act and breaches of the Fair Trading Acts in NSW and Victoria. She also found that Christie's had engaged in deceit and unconscionable conduct.In most cases,== when a buyer discovers they have bought a fake, the matter is settled quietly and the painting disappears from view. This is what happened in relation to three fake Brett Whiteleys that were passed off as real between 2007 and 2010.Ms McBride, however, did not discover that her painting was a fake for almost a decade. It hung in pride of place in her home and was much admired. But when she went to sell it, another auction house sounded the alarm.

In the course of preparing for the trial, she discovered that Christie's suspected soon after they sold her the artwork in 2000 that the painting was "problematic".They consulted experts in Melbourne, who confirmed it was probably fake. ==Yet, rather than tell Ms McBride, Christie's instead proceeded to sell another fake Tucker at their next auction.==

Justice Bergen rejected Christie's claim that Ms McBride was barred from bringing an action because more than five years had passed since the sale. ==In the case of a forgery, the cause of action arises when the defect is discovered,== she ruled.Justice Bergin also found that Ms McBride was entitled to damages over a separate claim against her agent, Ms Sharp, arising out of the sale of a Jeffrey Smart painting.

John Helmer: Auction House Bonhams, Sued Over Frauds ...

Mar 25, 2015 - **Bonhams** has been **selling** itself, according to the Financial Times, ... in a London court over Christie's in the case of a **fake** Kustodiev **painting**, ...

1. **More fakes at auction? - Art History News - by Bendor Grosvenor**

   Mar 21, 2012 - A leading Greek collector is suing Sotheby's over two alleged **fakes**. ... set a record price for the **artist** when he paid £670,100 for The Virgin and Child ... I doubt anyone really thinks a major auction house like Sotheby's knowingly **sells fakes**. ... Rumours of widespread forgery began in 2008 when **Bonhams** ...

1. **Mexico Says Bonhams Sold Fake Antiquities - artnet News**

   Nov 13, 2014 - Mexico's National Institute of Anthropology and History (INAH) has accused **Bonhams** New York of **selling** 29 **fake** pre-Columbian pieces in an ..

heres the fake from sotheby's (top middle) in this group. Sticks out pretty obvious. The edges of the dress and that hideous oversized bow !!! I reported it to a few authorities,

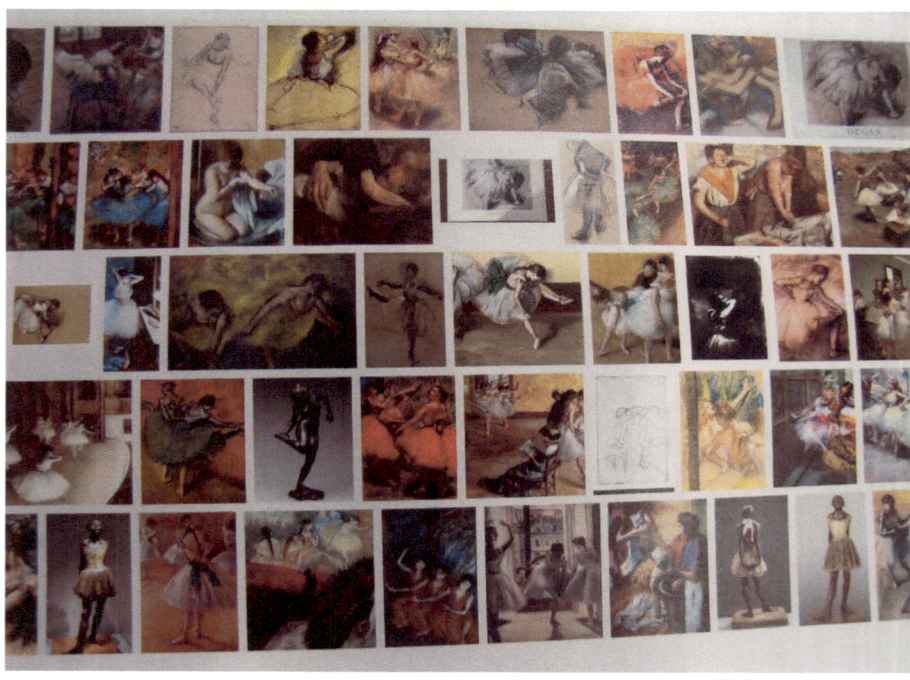

because it is VERY CRIMINAL to have this documented back in the 1880s. And then documented in published reference books !! WHOA>>> who's the mastermind behind this fraud ?? And now we have probable cause to believe there are more.

Here is a recent find today Feb 24th 2020, of which I also believe to be a fake. This is the best picture I was able to transfer, but there is the link for a better view.

https://www.sothebys.com/en/auctions/ecatalogue/2019/impressionist-modern-art-day-n10148/lot.120.html?locale=en

- IMPRESSIONIST & MODERN ART DAY SALE
EVERYTHING YOU CAN IMAGINE IS REAL: PROPERTY FROM AN IMPORTANT PRIVATE EUROPEAN COLLECTION

Edgar Degas
DANSEUSE À L'ÉVENTAIL
Estimate 300,000 — 500,000 USD **LOT SOLD.** 487,500 USD

PROVENANCE

Ambroise Vollard, Paris
O'Hana Gallery, London
Private Collection, Europe
Sale: Trianon Palace, Versailles, June 6, 1963
Sale: Galerie Motte, Geneva, November 2, 1971, lot 27
Acquired at the above sale

EXHIBITED>oh wow its in a book, that must mean its genuine !!

Martigny, Foundation Pierre Gianadda, *Degas*, 1993, no. 67, illustrated in the catalogue
London, O'Hana Gallery, *Summer Exhibition of Paintings and Sculpture of the Nineteenth and Twentieth Centuries*, 1962, n.n.

LITERATURE>oh WOW !!

Ambroise Vollard, *98 Reproductions signées par Degas, peintures, pastels, dessins et estampes*, Paris, 1914, illustrated pl. XCIV
Paul-André Lemoisne, *Degas et son oeuvre*, vol. III, New York & London, 1984, no. 1225, illustrated p. 711

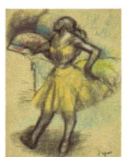

head looks small and neck is short also !!

CONDITION REPORT: >>and no garuntee of authenticity

The work is in very good condition. The sheet has been laid down to a card which has been adhered to a mount. The sheet is lightly time stained overall. There are a few minor nicks and losses and a minor line of mat staining to the bottom edge of the sheet, which are not visible when framed. There is a flattened crease along the top edge. There are some scattered spots of foxing and media staining throughout the sheet, commensurate with age. The pigments and colors are bright and fresh.

In response to your inquiry, we are pleased to provide you with a general report of the condition of the property described above. Since we are not professional conservators or restorers, we urge you to consult with a restorer or conservator of your choice who will be better able to provide a detailed, professional report. Prospective buyers should inspect each lot to satisfy themselves as to condition and must understand that any statement made by Sotheby's is merely a subjective qualified opinion.

NOTWITHSTANDING THIS REPORT OR ANY DISCUSSIONS CONCERNING CONDITION OF A LOT, ALL LOTS ARE OFFERED AND SOLD "AS IS" IN ACCORDANCE WITH THE CONDITIONS OF SALE PRINTED IN THE CATALOGUE

here is a larger pic taken with my cell phone, this work is an absolute shambles !! the entire face is fucked up, has a chin like a man and shaggy dog hair, Where's the right arm? Oh is that it?,, The shape thats not shaded black like the left arm? I like the way that hand is holding the fan !!! LOL !! thats really out of whack. and then

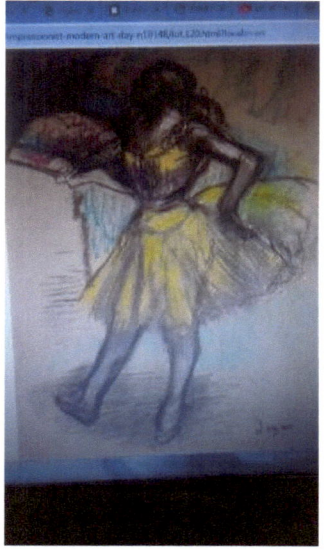

showing a bald spot on top of the head ???!!! this is an outrage to claim Edgar Degas created such a work !!, and executed in 1895-1900?? absolutely preposterous !. Although the forger has the signature well copied but the entirety of the subject is a total fraud in my opinion, Degas was using pastel mixtures that were well his repertoire by the mid to late 1870s. He did not scribble up faces !!! with a black chalk !!! this is CRAZY !!! AND WHAT'S EVEN CRAZIER IS THE DOCUMENTATION OF THIS monstrosity IS FRAUD & FAKE. What are we dealing with here?, A crime syndicate ?? Do they have their own studio ?? how many family generations continue these fake provenances ? This was done on paper>> What kind of paper ? Does anybody know Degas' paper types? I think it's very important.

Maybe the people deserve to be ripped off if they are that DUMB !!!, or maybe not ? I would surely expect a sworn notarized authentication when spending this kind of loot.

It is all becoming more so evident to me now as the years have passed that the auction houses are indeed have quite an expertise in the field of selling forgeries. The false and misleading statements, the hype, added with distracting historical facts to add to the belief that what is being sold is genuine but then there is no garuntee !! and the pumping up with well strategic sales pitches to the questionable artworks is surely an **"expertise"** in itself. Why would they want my genuine Edgar Degas mixed media painting when the evidence would surely expose what they have been selling the past 100 years ?? therefore everybody that had purchased an artwork allegedly created by Edgar Degas would find out they had bought a fake and there would be a domino effect of lawsuits. This is what I sincerely think. I also think certain auction houses have their own studio and paid off artists to create these fakes and also the Experts who have the "know how" to get these fakes documented and make a paper-trail of provenances, THUS AND create the lie that "provenance is the primary requirement for authenticity".. BRAVO BRAVO nicely done... But myself and others which own Genuine works are shunned away and refused to be given a chance because I now see how they have the market covered. These are just three fakes of which I found the third one this morning 02/24/2020, in about 15 minutes while trying to find a disclosure for garunteeing an artwork from sotheby's. I do know my Degas artworks concearning pastels very well. Seeing how I have even corrected the experts many times.

Lets take a look at some pastel mixtures on MY Degas taken with a 5 megapixel camera. And this is normal behavior for Edgar Degas to use them. As the national gallery of london stated there was a homade soap mixture made from glycerin Degas' even used, but one is yet to be found. I have my Degas artwork and ALL the auction houses avoid it for some reason. Yeah, I know why too.

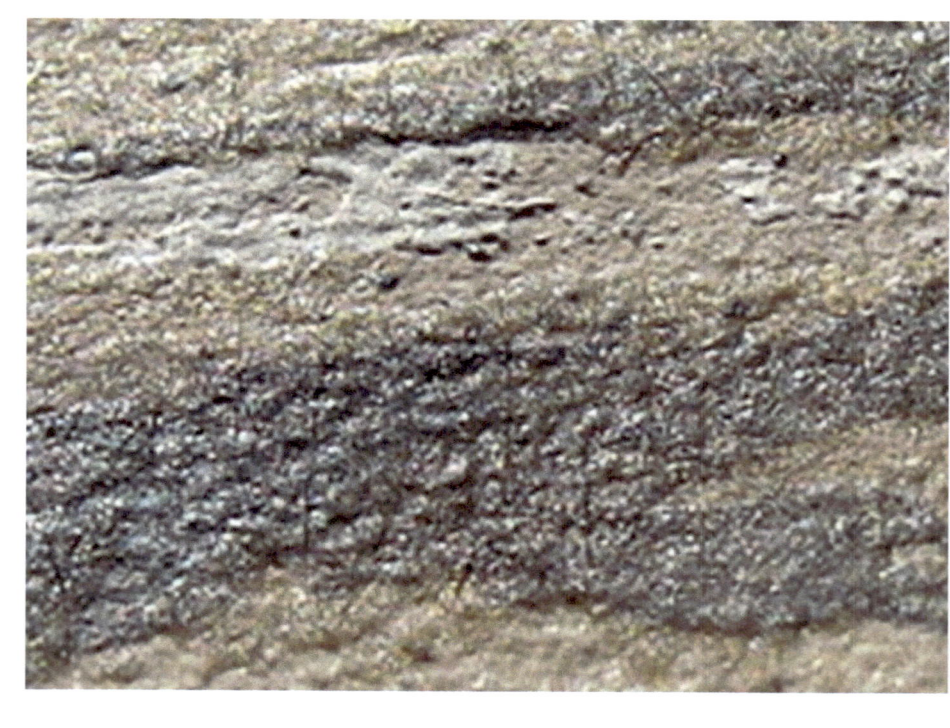

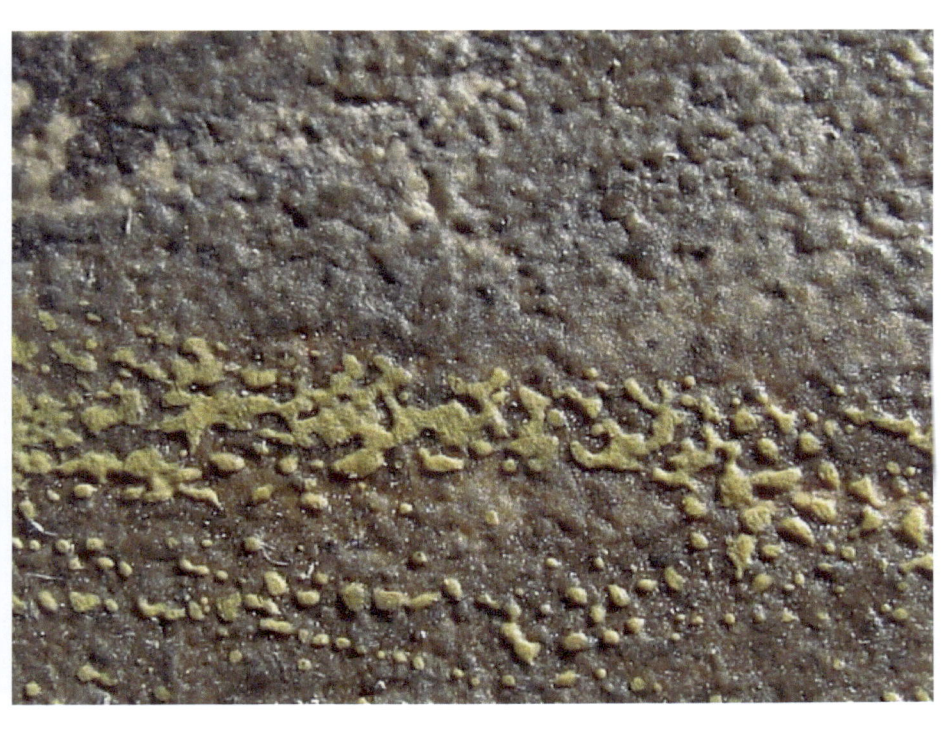

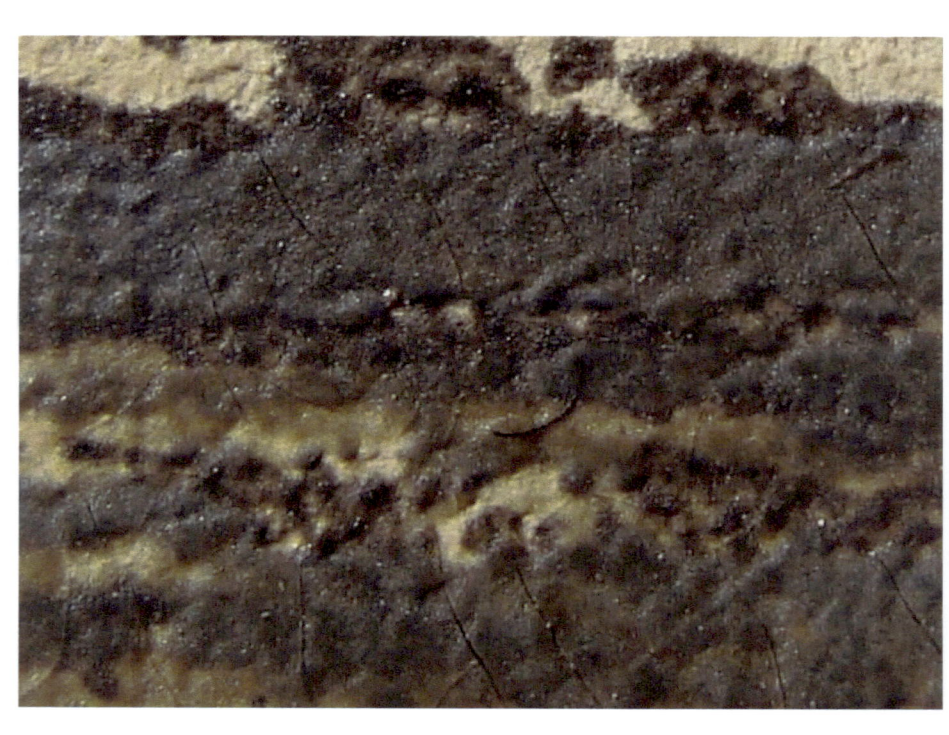

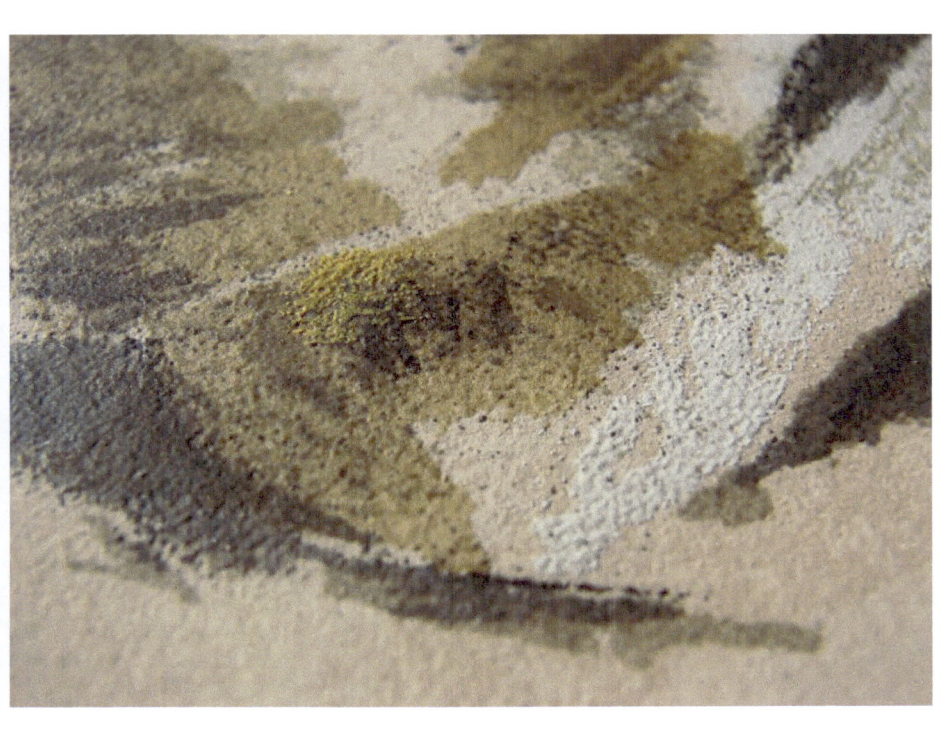

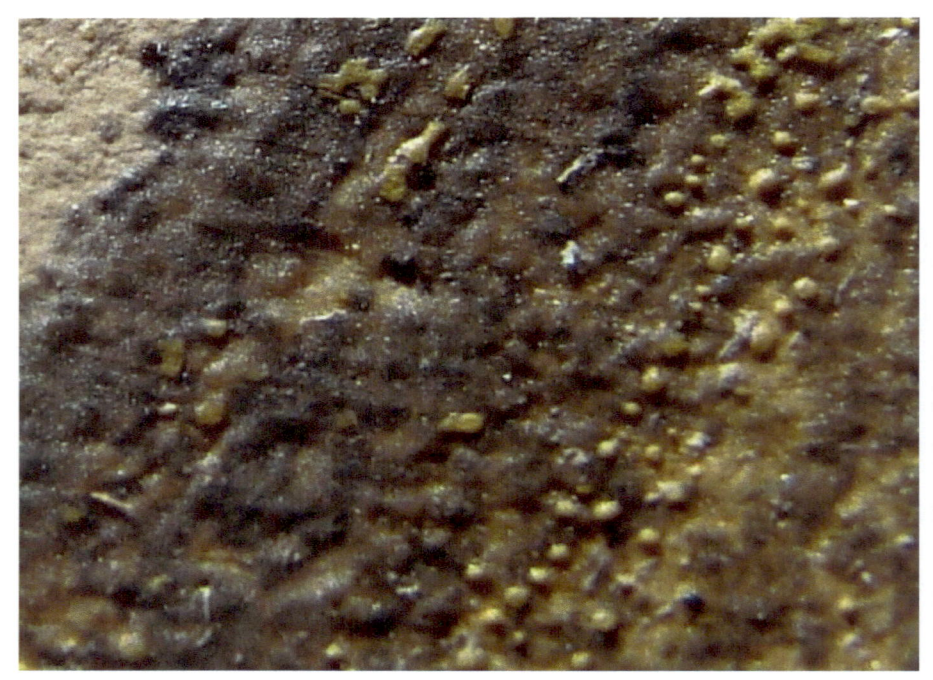

This is the media from my Edgar Degas mixed media

While my Degas artwork is in perfect harmony with style, photographic evidence, and many many aspects of being correct but it is not accepted. Is this some kind of a bad dream? Can anybody wake me up

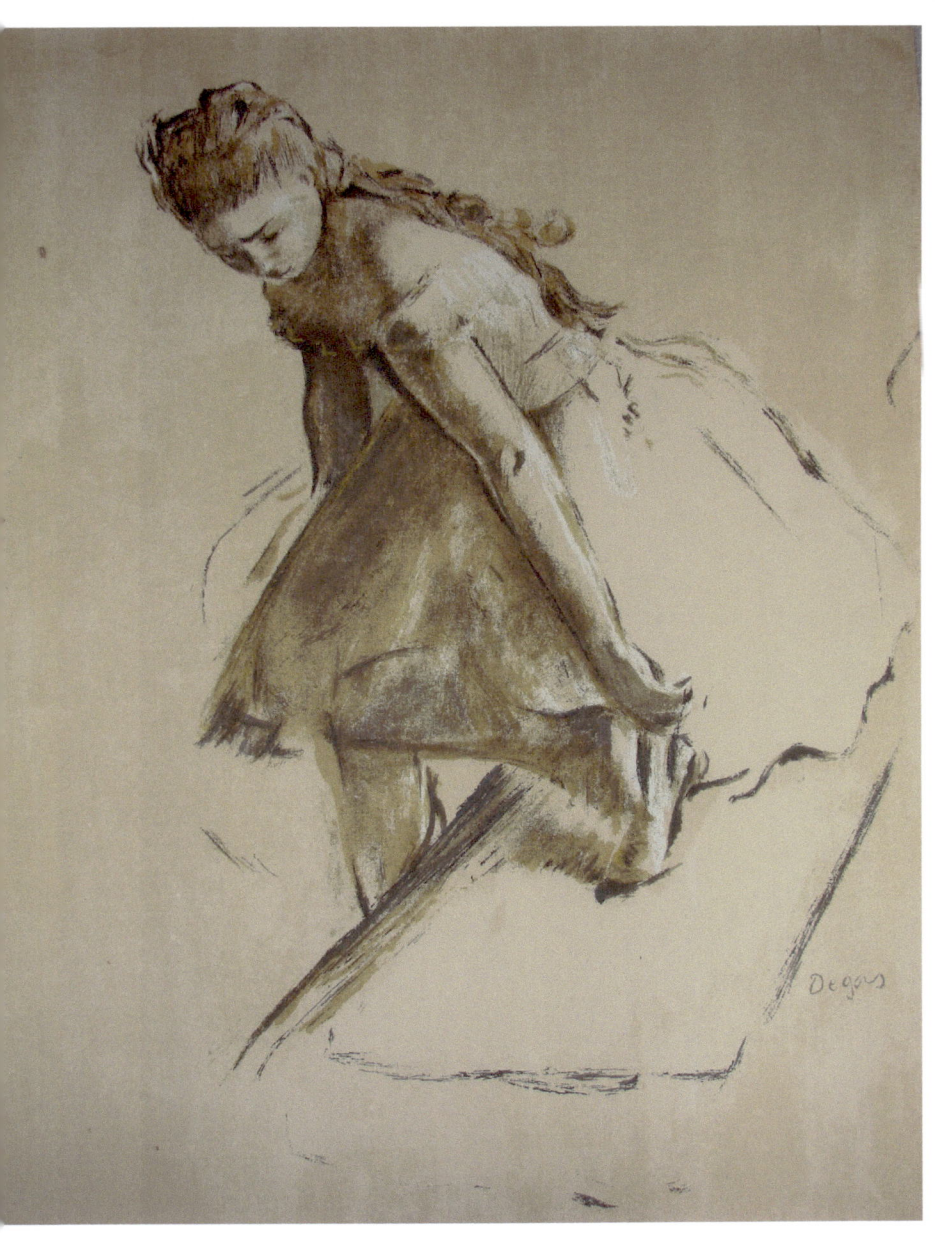

Picture taken in sunlight. Used sony cybershot DHS-2, 5 mgpxl with karl zeiss lens 12X zoom

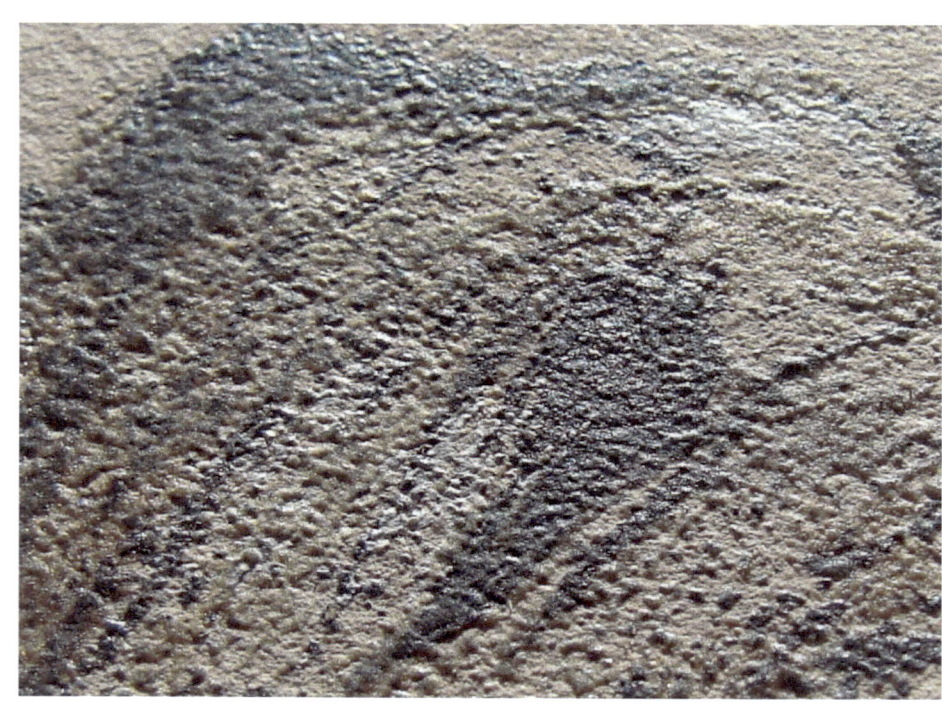

You should see all the BULLSHIT responses I've collected from the experts, saying this media is a collagraph, print, mechanically made, stencil, Absolutely ludicrous what they have told me !!!!!

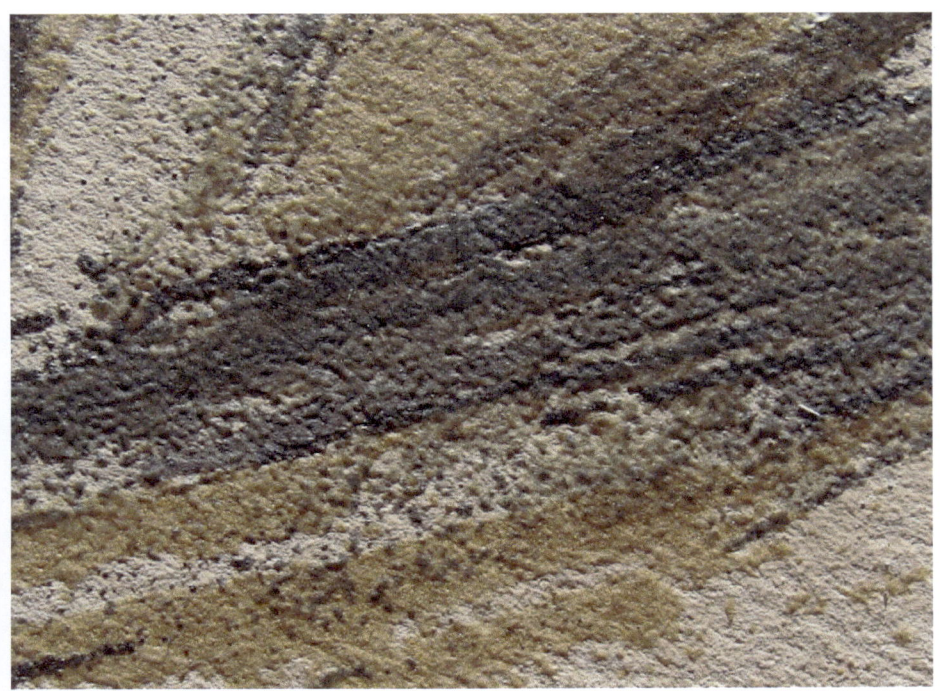

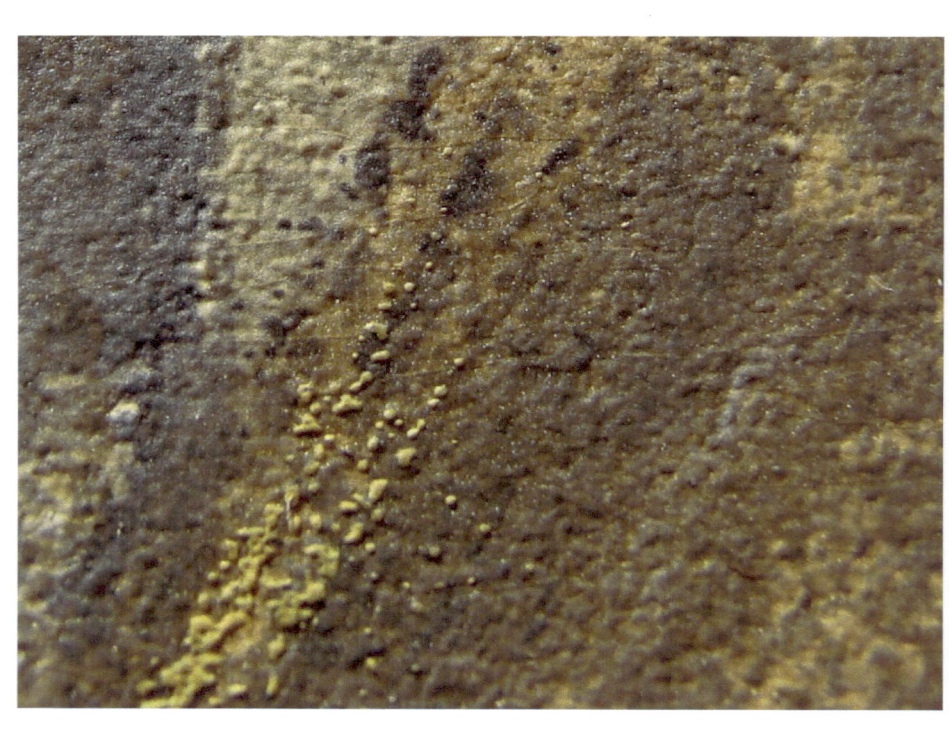

Fixative on top

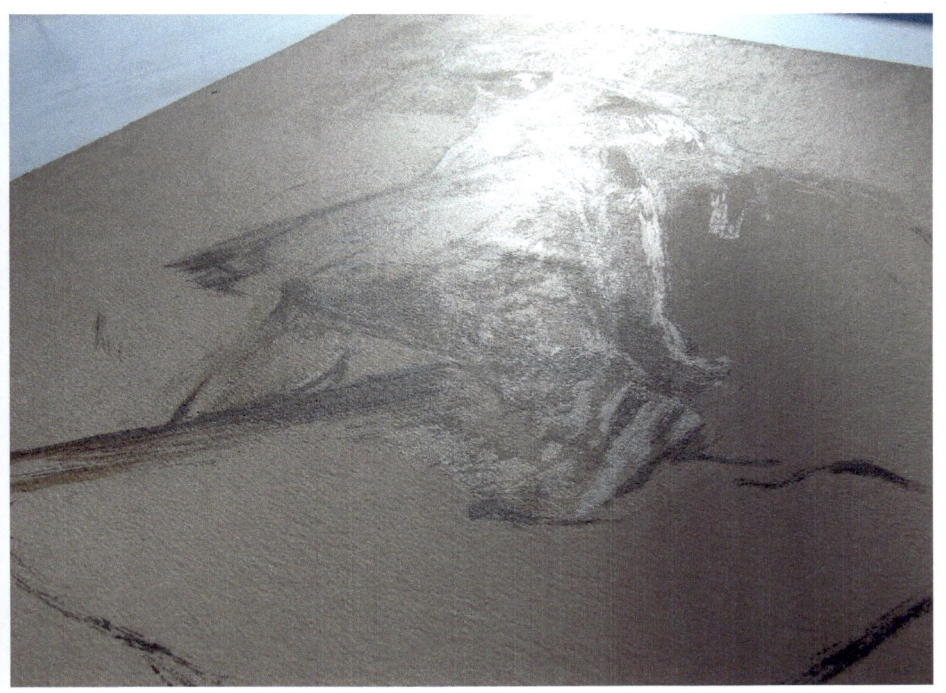

Why doesnt the auction houses show pictures like mine ?? In this picture shows Degas' fixative on the surface. This was VERY TYPICAL of his style !! Although you MAY HEAR OR SEE a report on fixative,,,,,,,,,,,,,,,,,wheres the fuckin picture?? And then show me the composition analysis of Degas' ingredients. This should be required on ALL Degas' works !!!!

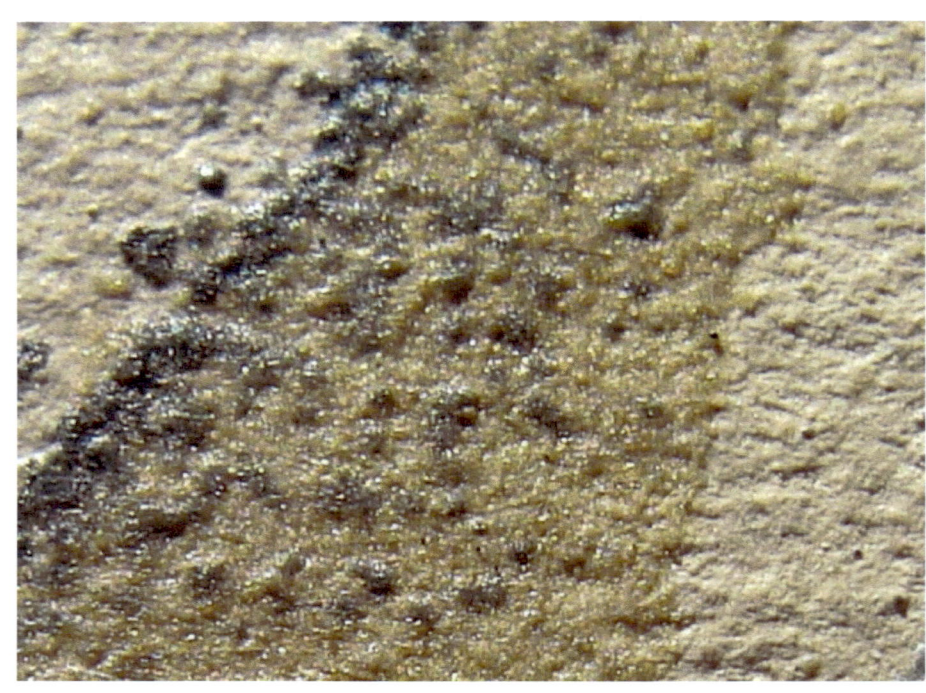

Very interesting mixture !!! I cant wait to get mine into a lab !! This is EXACTLY what Degas was doing>>> was his own creation of recipies and experiments. Yes this is on my Degas painting.

Check out this one I found on Sotheby's website this morning [feb 24]. As we know now from the aforementioned facts of Degas' style and use of media, here we have a pastel drawing aledgedly executed in 1880 from a "distinguished collection"? Haha

https://www.sothebys.com/en/auctions/ecatalogue/2019/impressionist-modern-art-day-n10068/lot.367.html

What caught my attention was the overweight chubby ballerina. After closer inspection there are no knee caps and the left leg looks like rubber, the hands arent right, the neck is short and it gives the appearance of a dwarf or midget ballerina.There is no elegance and its SLOPPY !! The pastel drawings as I reiterate Degas WAS BORED WITH !! ==He was using mixtures at the time of 1880 certainly. This work isn't as blatant as the others but EXTREMELY QUESTIONABLE, and in my opinion IS a forgery.== And again what is the paper type ?? All this money being spent and nobody cares about the paper. The condition report is speculation and common knowladge as I see a commonality used with other condition reports, and there is NO SWORN STATEMENT OF AUTHENTICITY. The provenance doesnt mean shit as the prior fakes all have fake provenances. This is quite serious.

Pic taken with my phone, see link above of actual listing

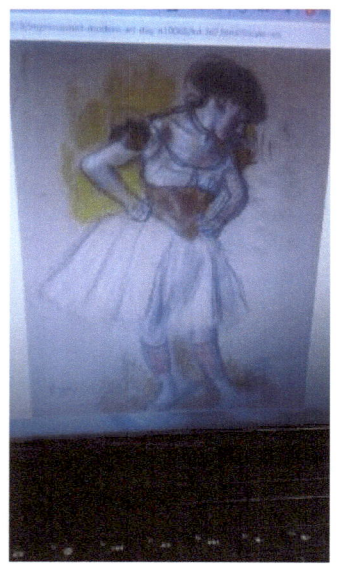
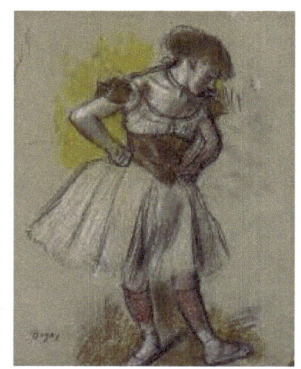

Edgar Degas
1834 - 1917
DANSEUSE

Signed *Degas* (lower left)
Charcoal and pastel on paper 11 7/8 by 9 1/2 in.
30 by 24.1 cm
Executed *circa* 1880.

READ CONDITION REPORTSALEROOM NOTICE

PROVENANCE

Jeanne Fèvre, Nice (the artist's niece; and sold: Galerie Charpentier, Paris, June 12, 1934, lot 100)Really? Wow !!, How are they documenting these works so long ago?? And again no laboratory analysis of paper. Just words. And what about checking for a watermark ??
Private Collection (acquired *circa* the 1950s)
Thence by descent

LITERATURE

Paul-André Lemoisne, *Degas et son oeuvre*, vol. II, Paris, 1946, no. 604, illustrated p. 343.Is this the book published by paul brame? And this makes the artwork genuine?

Art forgers, however, often falsify information establishing the provenance of a work of art— forging receipts of sale, ownership marks, dealers' records, exhibition labels, and collectors' stamps. For this reason, provenance history is seldom accepted as the sole proof of authenticity for a work of art.

Unfortunately, numerous forged or otherwise misrepresented works of art are offered for sale with fake or questionable provenance at online auctions like E-Bay, at fixed-price art websites and at brick-and-mortar establishments, but nowhere is the proliferation of problem art and problem provenance more pervasive than at online auctions. In order to fool inexperienced buyers, unscrupulous sellers often state that they have provenance or documented ownership histories that they claim confirms the authenticity of their bogus art. In some cases, this concocted provenance appears to date all the way back to the artists themselves. From my research there are "criminal rings" faking signatures and provenances worldwide. New York is close to #1 on the list also, And with so many payoffs and kickbacks and grease jobs, people are easily paid to back up a story. It's that simple, and it's sickening why the art world demands something that's so prolifically and easily fabricated

Here's the next one !(Frankenstien's wife,LOL !)

Do they have a warehouse full of these ?? How did Degas create this artwork in 1900? (or create it AT ALL, without eyes or an ear), another drawn pastel on paper I see, and very ugly. As what these auctions are claiming is absolutely unbelievable. Especially to Someone like myself who knows and studied Degas' style and his changing his methods of working with pastel. This is incredible !! As all the facts in support stating Degas repertoire and methods were so far advanced than a mere "drawn pastel". All the facts I have provided from museum curators, various historians and publicated sources of high credibility,,,,,,,,,,,,,,,,,,,,,,,and Sotheby's is selling these garbage forgeries !! OMG.. the thought is staggering how many have been sold !! It's absolutely impossible Degas would have done this work of a blacked out face when he was so far advanced and making improvements on his works using his own mixtures, always pushing for newer and better creations. ==This pastel among the others I've shown ARE NOT his style. this is sickening..== and yet another faked provenance to accompany a fake artwork. They surely have a system going on. And they fuckin lie to me and other people saying ours are not genuine?? BECAUSE THEY HAVE THIER OWN SUPPLY WITH PRE-PREPARED FAKED PROVENANCES !!!
Check out that nose, & that face !!! are you kidding me ?? LOL !! look at the shape of the head. Degas was an expert of the human anatomy and studied Da vinci.

    still haven't found any mixed media pastels like Degas was known for. (only a few exist}, Where the hell are all the mixed-media pastels? And how are these fakes being documented so far back ??

Do the auction houses think they are that powerful to control everybody because I'll be goddamn if they're going to sell this shit that is blatant fakes and then refuse to look at my genuine masterpiece which has all the facts and relevance .

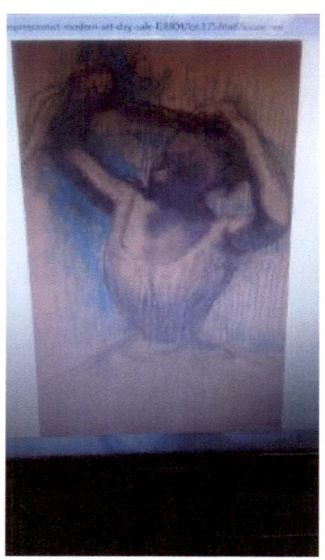 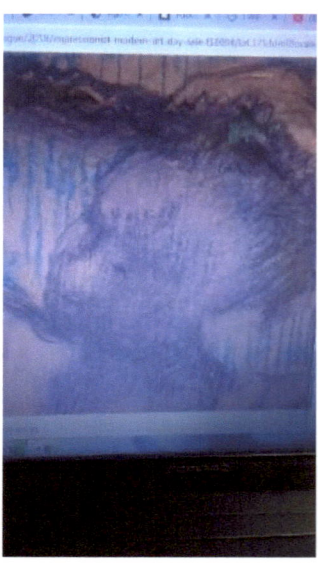

Here is the link for better pics on sotheby's website

https://www.sothebys.com/en/auctions/ecatalogue/2018/impressionist-modern-art-day-sale-l18004/lot.175.html?locale=en
IMPRESSIONIST & MODERN ART DAY SALE | 175

PROPERTY FROM A DISTINGUISHED PRIVATE EUROPEAN COLLECTION
Edgar Degas
DANSEUSE RAJUSTANT SA COIFFURE
Estimate 150,000 — 200,000 **GBP**

Edgar Degas

1834 - 1917
DANSEUSE RAJUSTANT SA COIFFURE

stamped *Degas* (lower left)
pastel and charcoal on paper laid down on board
56 by 36cm., 22 by 14 1/4 in.
Executed *circa* 1900.

PROVENANCE

Estate of the Artist (sale: Galerie Georges Petit, Paris, *Atelier Degas, 2ème Vente,* 11-13th December, 1918, lot 144)
Nunès et Fiquet, Paris
Adolphe Friedmann, Paris
Georges Friedmann, Paris (by descent from the above; sale: Artcurial, Paris, 20th April 2009, lot 41)
Private Collection, Paris
Acquired from the above by the present owner

LITERATURE

Paul-André Lemoisne, *Degas et son œuvre*, Paris, 1984, vol. III, no. 1385, illustrated p. 805

LOT NUMBER SALEROOM NOTICE
175 Please note that the medium for this work is pastel and charcoal on paper laid down on board.
CONDITION REPORT:
Executed on buff-coloured laid paper, **laid paper? What type? What weight? From which country?** laid down on board. There is a thin line of framer's tape running along all four edges, not visible when framed. There is a small pinhole to the upper left corner and there is a fine surface nick towards the lower left edge, not visible when framed. The sheet is time-stained and there are some scattered faint spots of foxing. This work is in overall good condition.
"In response to your inquiry, we are pleased to provide you with a general report of the condition of the property described above. Since we are not professional conservators or restorers, we urge you to consult with a restorer or conservator of your choice who will be better able to provide a detailed, professional report. Prospective buyers should inspect each lot to

satisfy themselves as to condition and must understand that any statement made by Sotheby's is merely a subjective, qualified opinion. Prospective buyers should also refer to any Important Notices regarding this sale, which are printed in the Sale Catalogue. Is there any garuntee of authenticity ? No X-ray imaging, and no chemical analysis of the pastel? NOTWITHSTANDING THIS REPORT OR ANY DISCUSSIONS CONCERNING A LOT, ALL LOTS ARE OFFERED AND SOLD AS IS" IN ACCORDANCE WITH THE CONDITIONS OF BUSINESS PRINTED IN THE SALE CATALOGUE.

The people sure are hoodwinked with those provenances, who could believe those are faked going way back ?? I DO. But the provenances can be argued, the facts provided of Degas' style and techniques cannot be argued, there's too much evidence from sources of high merit. So now I'm speaking about a crime syndicate, sure does make sence to me. With my Degas painting and other private collectors with their artworks all shunned by the auction houses. And yet we private people out here seperate from the artworld see all these artworks being sold with NO garuntees and "as is" disclosures, time passes and more fakes revealed. Just a repetitive cycle, but accelerating the number of forgeries discovered. And more cover-up stories made up by the experts and then more selling of fakes until they get caught again, same old cycle, and KICK out all the private collectors and dealers with their Genuine works, Because the Genuine works would surely expose the fakes, this is what they fear.

Control the information and control the beliefs,is why the major auction houses have the art world wrapped up in buying blatant forgeries. As I now see this website popped up called "Artnome" which claims to have all the works from Museum of Modern Art in their database as genuine,,,,, and no laboratory forensics or paper testing analysis has been done on these works. What about testing for watermarks? Didnt they know many of Degas' paper had watermarks ??

Throughout history it is documented a vast majority of artworks that are purchased by museums were forgeries and they are too embarrassed to speak about it so therefore how can "artnome" claim accuracy on there algorithm visual authenticity testing methods ?? It is surely not A-Reliable Source Four determining authorship of a specific work. And through the art world through the sales of works I have never seen a sworn statement under penalty of perjury stating that something is genuine Why Can't This be done and why can't they have a proper analysis ??

As these past years go by people ask me why doesn't Christie's or Sotheby's want to investigate my Edgar degas?, and I just reply they have their own Supply or I say the responses which they have given me are totally false

Are the fakes I exposed here in the "Artnome" database as genuine?? This gets even more crazier, more fiction and less fact in their "controlled information" I did contact artnome 3 times on their website and they never responded to me and there is no phone number. Very strange indeed. Well myself, I am an investigator, I dont give a dam who says what, I rely on the facts and not fabricated hype. I dont give a dam about who has big money and is claiming whatever, they are so manipulative. These are just a few I have uncovered for now and I'm sure there are plenty more forgeries to be found.

As you can see the next pictures show that Edgar Degas DID KNOW HOW to draw a face, a hand, a nose, a knee cap. He was vary familiar with the human anatomy. The previous work shown with the blacked out face and head shaped like a gourd and also that dis-proportioned nose, Degas could HAVE NEVER created, and especially in 1900 ??!! This is so criminal,,,,,I don't understand why this has been going on for so long??? Maybe because the experts control the documenting of these forgeries ? And the people believe it?
Yes indeed, control of information is control of the mind & beliefs.

http://www.arthistory.upenn.edu/ashmolean/Degas/Degas_entry.html

1880, smaller one is mid 1870s

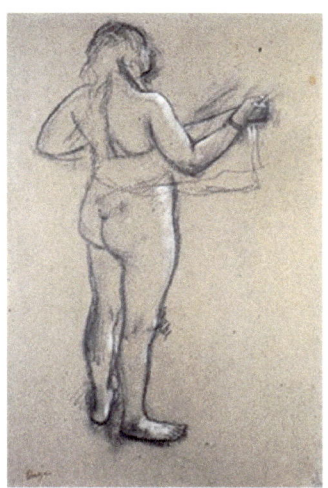

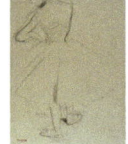

==Degas drew faces like this, and not like a monster. And she even has ears and eyes !!!head and neck proportion is correct also, not at all like the one fake I showed with the small head scribbled in black, why would Degas scribble faces in black when he could make them so beautiful like this one ? People need to WAKE UP !!! seriously !!==

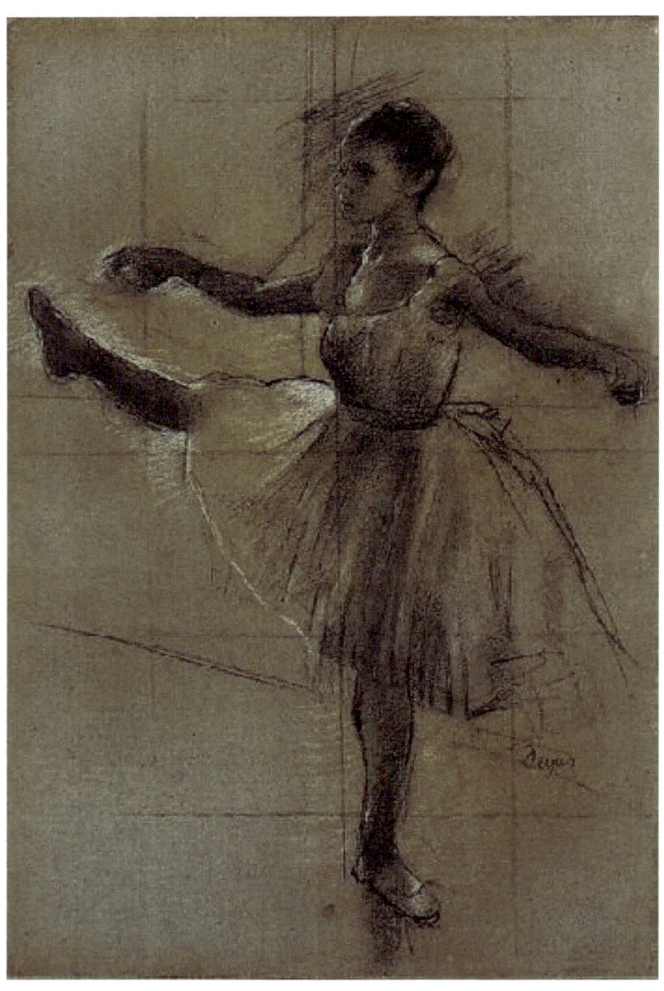

When is scholarly research and technical evidence considered fact or presumptions ??It should be considered with the amount of factual memorandum in support. (This does not mean shady and misleading word trickery from lab Doctors or other fancy titles which DO TELL LIES !! I already have shown Dr. Libby's report is such a falsley stated BS-story !!) Which means NOT ASSUMED. These "provenances" are all assumed, there are no facts to prove authentic, no sworn affidavit, and we all know and see other forgeries well documented back in time.

I'm having a real problem trying to understand something that who made up the rule that an artwork shall not be accepted as genuine without provenance. I'm also having a hard time understanding why artworks are being sold as genuine when they do not coincide with the facts of repertoire and style of authorship.

My insinuations and accusations to say something is Criminal is based on these experts with all their years of experience and education to allow these Works to be sold , and a man like me comes along which is a high school dropout, studying his own artwork, and simply compares the facts to the artwork by extensive research. I have found out the facts are greatly in support of the Edgar Degas that I own, but also in severe contradiction to what is being sold at the auction houses as genuine. Therefore it is my duty to report the truth as I have found it . I have not much to say about the museums as they are not in motive for profits and GREED. If they own a forgery it is clearly by mistake.

<u>My point of view contends that another STANDARD of authentication is needed to show tangible and factual proof,</u>
<u>Authenticity is a requirement for inscription upon the UNESCO World Heritage List.</u>
[4]According to the *Nara Document on Authenticity*, it can be expressed through 'form and design; materials and substance; use and function; traditions and techniques; location and setting; spirit and feeling; and other internal and external factors.'[5][6]

In many cases, particularly works of art produced before the 20th century, it may be impossible to reconstruct the complete ownership history of a work of art. Many archives have suffered damage or dispersal through wars or natural disasters, and documentary materials are often lost or missing. Moreover, private owners may not have saved purchase records over the years, particularly for works of lesser monetary value; and dealers and galleries may no longer be in business. Even where such documents exist, it can be difficult for the researcher to obtain access to them. ==But yet the auction houses HAVE PERFECT RECORD OF EVERYTHING ?? Hhhmmm.==

The End,,,,,,,,,,,,,,,,until I find more,,,,,,,,,,,,,,,,,,,,,,,,

troy-joseph   antiquefineartt@aol.com

www.ingramcontent.com/pod-product-compliance
Lightning Source LLC
Chambersburg PA
CBHW040242220526
45473CB00001B/345